THIS JOURNAL BELONGS TO

_____

DATE

_____

We walk without fear,
full of hope and courage
and strength to do His will,
waiting for the endless good
which He is always giving as fast
as He can get us able to take it in.

GEORGE MACDONALD

COURAGE, DEAR HEART

*Y*ou are a beloved child of God, precious to Him
in every way. As you seek Him, He will show you
the mysteries of life and unfold His unique plans
for you—a life full of rich blessing and peaceful
assurance. God cares about you and knows all the
desires of your heart. He is as close as breathing.

Let this journal inspire you to express your thoughts,
record your prayers, embrace your dreams,
and listen to what God is saying to you.
Be strong in the Lord, and have courage, dear heart.

Let us come boldly to the throne of our gracious God. There we will receive his mercy, and we will find grace to help us when we need it most.

HEBREWS 4:16 NLT

If you have a special need today, focus your full attention on the goodness and greatness of your Father rather than on the size of your need. Your need is so small compared to His ability to meet it.

God is our refuge and strength, an ever-present help in trouble.
Therefore we will not fear.

PSALM 46:1-2 NIV

*D*o you believe that God is near? He wants you to. He wants you to know that He is in the midst of your world. Wherever you are as you read these words, He is present.... He's near. And He is more than near. He is active.

MAX LUCADO

Let all that I am wait quietly before God, for my hope is in him.

PSALM 62:5 NLT

Be still, and in the quiet moments, listen to the voice
of your heavenly Father. His words can renew your spirit....
No one knows you and your needs like He does.

JANET L. SMITH

*Y*ou will keep in perfect peace those whose minds are steadfast, because they trust in you. Trust in the LORD forever, for the LORD, the LORD himself, is the Rock eternal.

ISAIAH 26:3-4 NIV

All God's glory and beauty come from within, and there
He delights to dwell. His visits there are frequent, His conversation sweet,
His comforts refreshing, His peace passing all understanding.

THOMAS À KEMPIS

Taste and see that the LORD is good. Oh, the joys of those who take refuge in him! Fear the LORD, you his godly people, for those who fear him will have all they need.

PSALM 34:8-9 NLT

When God finds a soul that rests in Him and is not easily moved...
to this same soul He gives the joy of His presence.

CATHERINE OF GENOA

I'll take the hand of those who don't know the way, who can't see where they're going. I'll be a personal guide to them, directing them through unknown country. I'll be right there to show them what roads to take, make sure they don't fall into the ditch. These are the things I'll be doing for them—sticking with them, not leaving them for a minute.

ISAIAH 42:16 MSG

I would rather walk with God in the dark than go alone in the light.

MARY GARDINER BRAINARD

For you are my hiding place; you protect me from trouble.
You surround me with songs of victory. The Lord says, "I will guide you along
the best pathway for your life. I will advise you and watch over you."

Psalm 32:7-8 NLT

O Lord…let me not fear too much the storms and winds of my daily life,
and let me know that there is ebb and flow…but that the sea remains the sea.

HENRI J. M. NOUWEN

$\mathcal{D}$on't be afraid, I've redeemed you. I've called your name. You're mine.
When you're in over your head, I'll be there with you.
When you're in rough waters, you will not go down. When you're
between a rock and a hard place, it won't be a dead end—because I am GOD,
your personal God...your Savior. I paid a huge price for you...!
That's how much you mean to me! *That's* how much I love you!

ISAIAH 43:1-4 MSG

*L*ive for today but hold your hands open to tomorrow. Anticipate the future and its changes with joy. There is a seed of God's love in every event, every circumstance, every unpleasant situation in which you may find yourself.

BARBARA JOHNSON

How abundant are the good things that you have stored up for those who fear you, that you bestow in the sight of all, on those who take refuge in you.

PSALM 31:19 NIV

The goodness of God is infinitely more wonderful
than we will ever be able to comprehend.

A. W. TOZER

The LORD longs to be gracious to you; therefore he will rise up to show you compassion. For the LORD is a God of justice. Blessed are all who wait for him!

ISAIAH 30:18 NIV

*G*od still draws near to us in the ordinary, commonplace, everyday
experiences and places.... He comes in surprising ways.

HENRY GARIEPY

I love the LORD because he hears my voice and my prayer for mercy.
Because he bends down to listen, I will pray as long as I have breath!

Whoso draws nigh to God
One step through doubtings dim,
God will advance a mile
In blazing light to him.

So we fix our eyes not on what is seen, but on what is unseen, since what is seen is temporary, but what is unseen is eternal.

2 CORINTHIANS 4:18 NIV

God may be invisible, but He's in touch. You may not be able to see Him,
but He is in control. And that includes you—your circumstances.
That includes what you've just lost. That includes what you've just gained.
That includes all of life—past, present, future.

CHARLES R. SWINDOLL

I can do all things through Christ who strengthens me.

PHILIPPIANS 4:13 NKJV

Whatever the circumstances, whatever the call...
His strength will be your strength in your hour of need.

BILLY GRAHAM

I am certain that God, who began the good work within you, will continue his work until it is finally finished on the day when Christ Jesus returns.

PHILIPPIANS 1:6 NLT

God, who has led you safely on so far, will lead you on to the end.
Be altogether at rest in the loving holy confidence,
which you ought to have in His heavenly Providence.

FRANCIS DE SALES

*H*e will feed his flock like a shepherd.
He will carry the lambs in his arms, holding them close to his heart.

ISAIAH 40:11 NLT

God never abandons anyone on whom He has set His love; nor does Christ, the good shepherd, ever lose track of His sheep.

My Presence will go with you, and I will give you rest.

EXODUS 33:14 NIV

My Lord God, I have no idea where I am going. I do not see the road ahead of me. I cannot know for certain where it will end.... But I believe that the desire to please You does in fact please You. And I hope I have that desire in all that I am doing. I hope that I will never do anything apart from that desire. And I know that if I do this, You will lead me by the right road though I may know nothing about it.

THOMAS MERTON

*B*less the LORD, O my soul, and forget not all His benefits:
who forgives all your iniquities, who heals all your diseases,
who redeems your life from destruction, who crowns you with
lovingkindness and tender mercies, who satisfies your mouth
with good things, so that your youth is renewed like the eagle's.

PSALM 103:2-5 NKJV

The goodness of God is infinitely more wonderful
than we will ever be able to comprehend.

A. W. Tozer

God is sheer mercy and grace; not easily angered,
he's rich in love.... As high as heaven is over the earth,
so strong is his love to those who fear him.

PSALM 103:8, 11 MSG

The Lord's chief desire is to reveal Himself to you and, in order
for Him to do that, He gives you abundant grace. The Lord gives you
the experience of enjoying His presence. He touches you, and His touch
is so delightful that, more than ever, you are drawn inwardly to Him.

MADAME JEANNE GUYON

If I rise on the wings of the dawn, if I settle on the far side of the sea,
even there your hand will guide me, your right hand will hold me fast.

PSALM 139:9-10 NIV

God guides us, despite our uncertainties and our vagueness,
even through our failings and mistakes.... He leads us step by step,
from event to event. Only afterwards...when we survey the whole
progress of our lives, do we experience the feeling of having been led
without knowing it, the feeling that God has mysteriously guided us.

PAUL TOURNIER

*K*now therefore that the Lord your God is God; he is the faithful God,
keeping his covenant of love to a thousand generations
of those who love him and keep his commands.

DEUTERONOMY 7:9 NIV

The first time God gave Himself a name in the Bible, He called Himself the "I Am." He is the one who is from eternity to eternity. He is the one who never changes. He is the one who calls you by name and numbers the hairs on your head.

JOANIE GARBORG

*B*e anxious for nothing, but in everything by prayer and supplication,
with thanksgiving, let your requests be made known to God;
and the peace of God, which surpasses all understanding,
will guard your hearts and minds through Christ Jesus.

PHILIPPIANS 4:6-7 NKJV

The God of peace gives perfect peace to those
whose hearts are stayed upon Him.

CHARLES H. SPURGEON

I am leaving you with a gift—peace of mind and heart. And the peace I give is a gift the world cannot give. So don't be troubled or afraid.

JOHN 14:27 NLT

I will let God's peace infuse every part of today. As the chaos swirls and life's demands pull at me on all sides, I will breathe in God's peace that surpasses all understanding. He has promised that He would set within me a peace too deeply planted to be affected by unexpected or exhausting demands. Life from the Center is a life of unhurried peace and power. It is simple. It is serene.... We need not get frantic. He is at the helm. And when our little day is done, we lie down quietly in peace, for all is well.

THOMAS R. KELLY

Ah, Sovereign LORD, you have made the heavens and the earth by your great power and outstretched arm. Nothing is too hard for you.

JEREMIAH 32:17 NIV

*G*od cares for the world He created, from the rising of a nation to the falling of the sparrow. Everything in the world lies under the watchful gaze of His providential eyes, from the numbering of the days of our life to the numbering of the hairs on our head. When we look at the world from that perspective, it produces within us a response of reverence.

KEN GIRE

*T*he LORD bless you, and keep you;
The LORD make His face shine on you,
And be gracious to you;
The LORD lift up His countenance on you,
And give you peace.

NUMBERS 6:24-26 NASB

Calm me, O Lord, as you stilled the storm,
Still me, O Lord, keep me from harm.
Let all the tumult within me cease,
Enfold me, Lord, in your peace.

CELTIC TRADITIONAL

I trust in your unfailing love. I will rejoice because you have rescued me.
I will sing to the LORD because he is good to me.

PSALM 13:5-6 NLT

God bless you and utterly satisfy your heart...with Himself.

AMY CARMICHAEL

*P*raise be to the name of God for ever and ever;
wisdom and power are his.... He reveals deep and hidden things;
he knows what lies in darkness, and light dwells with him.

DANIEL 2:20, 22 NIV

*K*now by the light of faith that God is present,
and be content with directing all your actions toward Him.

BROTHER LAWRENCE

*L*et the redeemed of the Lord say so.... They were hungry and thirsty; their soul fainted within them. Then they cried out to the Lord in their trouble; He delivered them out of their distresses.... Let them give thanks to the Lord for His lovingkindness...for He has satisfied the thirsty soul, and the hungry soul He has filled with what is good.

Psalm 107:2, 5-6, 8-9 NASB

God cannot give us a happiness and peace apart from Himself, because it is not there. There is no such thing.

C. S. LEWIS

Give your burdens to the LORD, and he will take care of you.
He will not permit the godly to slip and fall.

PSALM 55:22 NLT

*D*o not be afraid to enter the cloud that is settling down on your life.
God is in it. The other side is radiant with His glory.

L. B. COWMAN

I am the light of the world. Whoever follows me
will never walk in darkness, but will have the light of life.

JOHN 8:12 NIV

*G*uidance is a sovereign act. Not merely does God will to guide
us by showing us His way;...whatever mistakes we may make,
we shall come safely home. Slippings and strayings there will be,
no doubt, but the everlasting arms are beneath us; we shall be caught,
rescued, restored. This is God's promise; this is how good He is.
And our self-distrust, while keeping us humble, must not cloud
the joy with which we lean on our faithful covenant God.

J. I. PACKER

Be sure of this: I am with you always, even to the end of the age.

MATTHEW 28:20 NLT

We are always in the presence of God.... There is never a non-sacred moment! His presence never diminishes. Our awareness of His presence may falter, but the reality of His presence never changes.

MAX LUCADO

*T*hey cried out to the LORD in their trouble, and he brought them out of their distress. He stilled the storm to a whisper; the waves of the sea were hushed. They were glad when it grew calm, and he guided them to their desired haven.

PSALM 107:28-30 NIV

We must drink deeply from the very Source the deep calm and peace of interior quietude and refreshment of God, allowing the pure water of divine grace to flow plentifully and unceasingly from the Source itself.

MOTHER TERESA

*T*ake delight in the LORD, and he will give you the desires of your heart.
Commit your way to the LORD; trust in him and he will do this:
He will make your righteous reward shine like the dawn,
your vindication like the noonday sun.

PSALM 37:4-6 NIV

*T*rust the past to the mercy of God, the present to His love,
and the future to His Providence.

AUGUSTINE

*S*end me your light and your faithful care, let them lead me;
let them bring me to your holy mountain, to the place where you dwell.
Then will I go to the altar of God, to God, my joy and my delight.

PSALM 43:3-4 NIV

Heaven often seems distant and unknown, but if He
who made the road…is our guide, we need not fear to lose the way.

HENRY VAN DYKE

He heals the brokenhearted and binds up their wounds.... Great is our Lord, and abundant in power; his understanding is beyond measure.

PSALM 147:3, 5 ESV

The Lord promises to bind up the brokenhearted, to give relief and full deliverance to those whose spirits have been weighed down.

CHARLES R. SWINDOLL

Truly my soul finds rest in God; my salvation comes from him. Truly he is my rock and my salvation; he is my fortress, I will never be shaken.

PSALM 62:1-2 NIV

The thought of You stirs us so deeply that we cannot be content
unless we praise You, because You have made us for yourself
and our hearts find no peace until they rest in You.

AUGUSTINE

Your kingdom is an everlasting kingdom. You rule throughout all generations.
The LORD always keeps his promises; he is gracious in all he does.

PSALM 145:13 NLT

God is the God of promise. He keeps His word,
even when that seems impossible.

COLIN URQUHART

By day the LORD directs his love, at night his song
is with me—a prayer to the God of my life.

PSALM 42:8 NIV

*L*ife in the presence of God should be known to us in conscious experience.
It is a life to be enjoyed every moment of every day.

A. W. TOZER

*I*t is God who works in you to will and to act
in order to fulfill his good purpose.

PHILIPPIANS 2:13 NIV

What we need to know, of course, is not just that God exists, not just that beyond the steely brightness of the stars there is a cosmic intelligence... but that there is a God right here in the thick of our day-by-day lives who may not be writing messages about Himself in the stars but in one way or another is trying to get messages through our blindness.

FREDERICK BUECHNER

The Lᴏʀᴅ is my shepherd, I lack nothing. He makes me lie down in green pastures, he leads me beside quiet waters, he refreshes my soul.

PSALM 23:1-3 NIV

*H*ave confidence in God's mercy, for when you think
He is a long way from you, He is often quite near.

THOMAS À KEMPIS

The LORD watches over you—the LORD is your shade at your right hand;
he sun will not harm you by day, not the moon by night. The LORD will
keep you from all harm—he will watch over your life; the LORD will
watch over your coming and going both now and forevermore.

PSALM 121:5-8 NIV

*G*od is here. I have joyously discovered that He is always
  "up to something" in my life, and I am learning
to quit second-guessing Him and simply trust the process.

GLORIA GAITHER

The steadfast love of the Lord never ceases; his mercies never
come to an end; they are new every morning; great is your faithfulness.

LAMENTATIONS 3:22-23 ESV

We have a Father in heaven who is almighty, who loves His children
as He loves His only-begotten Son, and whose very joy and delight
it is to...help them at all times and under all circumstances.

Hear my cry, O God; give heed to my prayer. From the end of the earth I call to You when my heart is faint; lead me to the rock that is higher than I. For You have been a refuge for me, a tower of strength against the enemy.

PSALM 61:1-3 NASB

Nothing in your daily life is so insignificant and so inconsequential that God will not help you by answering your prayer.

OLE HALLESBY

Can a mother forget the baby at her breast and have no compassion on the child she has borne? Though she may forget, I will not forget you! See, I have engraved you on the palms of my hands.

ISAIAH 49:15-16 NIV

When I walk by the wayside, He is along with me.... Amid all my forgetfulness of Him, He never forgets me.

THOMAS CHALMERS

Now all glory to God, who is able to keep you from falling away and will bring you with great joy into his glorious presence without a single fault. All glory to him who alone is God.

JUDE 1:24-25 NLT

Today Jesus is working just as wonderful works as when He created the heaven and the earth. His wondrous grace, His wonderful omnipotence, is for His child who needs Him and who trusts Him, even today.

CHARLES HURLBURT AND T. C. HORTON

The LORD will give strength unto His people;
the LORD will bless His people with peace.

PSALM 29:11 NKJV

Can we find a friend so faithful,
Who will all our sorrows share?
Jesus knows our every weakness:
Take it to the Lord in prayer.

GEORGE SCRIVEN

You go before me and follow me.
You place your hand of blessing on my head.

PSALM 139:5 NLT

*B*efore me, even as behind, God is, and all is well.

The Lord is my rock and my fortress and my deliverer, my God, my rock,
in whom I take refuge; my shield and the horn of my salvation,
my stronghold. I call upon the Lord, who is worthy to be praised.

PSALM 18:2-3 NASB

*W*e could never learn to be brave and patient,
if there were only joy in the world.

HELEN KELLER

*You, Lord, are a compassionate and gracious God,
slow to anger, abounding in love and faithfulness.*

PSALM 86:15 NIV

God is every moment totally aware of each one of us. Totally aware
in intense concentration and love.... No one passes through
any area of life, happy or tragic, without the attention of God with him.

EUGENIA PRICE

*Even when I walk through the darkest valley,
I will not be afraid, for you are close beside me.*

PSALM 23:4 NLT

*T*herefore will I trust You always though I may seem to be lost
and in the shadow of death. I will not fear, for You are ever with me.
And You will never leave me to face my perils alone.

THOMAS MERTON

Give all your worries and cares to God, for he cares about you.

1 PETER 5:7 NLT

*B*ecause God is responsible for our welfare, we are told to cast all our care upon Him, for He cares for us. God says, "I'll take the burden— don't give it a thought—leave it to Me." God is keenly aware that we are dependent upon Him for life's necessities.

BILLY GRAHAM

*A*re not five sparrows sold for two pennies? Yet not one of them is forgotten by God. Indeed, the very hairs of your head are all numbered. Don't be afraid; you are worth more than many sparrows.

LUKE 12:6-7 NIV

God knows everything about us. And He cares about everything.
Moreover, He can manage every situation. And He loves us!
Surely this is enough to open the wellsprings of joy.

HANNAH WHITALL SMITH

*Y*our love, LORD, reaches to the heavens, your faithfulness to the skies....
How priceless is your unfailing love, O God! People take refuge
in the shadow of your wings. They feast on the abundance of your house;
you give them drink from your river of delights. For with you
is the fountain of life; in your light we see light.

PSALM 36:5, 7-9 NIV

When God has become...our refuge and our fortress, then we can reach out to Him in the midst of a broken world and feel at home while still on the way.

HENRI J. M. NOUWEN

*M*y God is changeless in his love for me, and he will come and help me.

PSALM 59:10 TLB

At the very heart and foundation of all God's dealings with us, however dark and mysterious they may be, we must dare to believe in and assert the infinite, unmerited, and unchanging love of God.

L. B. COWMAN

My God will meet all your needs according to
the riches of his glory in Christ Jesus.

PHILIPPIANS 4:19 NIV

*G*od wants nothing from us except our needs, and these furnish Him with room to display His bounty when He supplies them freely.... Not what I have, but what I do not have, is the first point of contact between my soul and God.

CHARLES H. SPURGEON

I keep my eyes always on the LORD.
With him at my right hand, I will not be shaken.

PSALM 16:8 NIV

The "air" which our souls need also envelops all of us at all times
and on all sides. God is round about us...on every hand,
with many-sided and all-sufficient grace.

OLE HALLESBY

I am always with you; you hold me by my right hand.

PSALM 73:23 NIV

*T*he God who created, names, and numbers the stars in the heavens
also numbers the hairs of my head.... He pays attention
to very big things and to very small ones. What matters to me
matters to Him, and that changes my life.

ELISABETH ELLIOT

*M*any, O LORD my God, are the wonders which You have done,
and Your thoughts toward us; There is none to compare with You.
If I would declare and speak of them, they would be too numerous to count.

PSALM 40:5 NASB

God is in the details; God is in the moment.
God is in all that blurs by in a life.

ANN VOSKAMP

How great are your works, Lord, how profound your thoughts!

PSALM 92:5 NIV

*W*hat matters supremely is not the fact that I know God,
but the larger fact which underlies it—the fact that *He knows me*.
I am graven on the palms of His hands. I am never out of His mind.
All my knowledge of Him depends on His sustained initiative in knowing me.
I know Him because He first knew me, and continues to know me.

J. I. PACKER

*S*eek the L‍ord your God and you will find him,
if you search after him with all your heart and with all your soul.

DEUTERONOMY 4:29 ESV

When we allow God the privilege of shaping our lives,
we discover new depths of purpose and meaning.

Come to me, all of you who are weary and carry heavy burdens, and I will give you rest. Take my yoke upon you. Let me teach you, because I am humble and gentle at heart, and you will find rest for your souls. For my yoke is easy to bear, and the burden I give you is light.

MATTHEW 11:28-30 NLT

*G*od is waiting for us to come to Him with our needs.... God's throne room is always open.... Every single believer in the whole world could walk into the throne room all at one time, and it would not even be crowded.

CHARLES STANLEY

The everlasting God, the Lord...neither faints nor is weary.
His understanding is unsearchable. He gives power to the weak, and to those
who have no might He increases strength. Even the youths shall faint and be
weary, and the young men shall utterly fall, but those who wait on the Lord
shall renew their strength; they shall mount up with wings like eagles,
they shall run and not be weary, they shall walk and not faint.

Isaiah 40:28-31 NKJV

*O*ur strength often increases in proportion to the obstacles imposed upon it.

PAUL DE RAPIN

"*For* I know the plans I have for you," declares the Lord, "plans to prosper you and not to harm you, plans to give you hope and a future."

JEREMIAH 29:11 NIV

*Taken separately, the experiences of life can work harm and not good.
Taken together, they make a pattern of blessing and strength
the like of which the world does not know.*

V. RAYMOND EDMAN

I pray that out of his glorious riches he may strengthen
you with power through his Spirit in your inner being.

EPHESIANS 3:16 NIV

*W*hatever the circumstances, whatever the call...
His strength will be your strength in your hour of need.

BILLY GRAHAM

*M*y flesh and my heart may fail, but God is the strength of my heart
and my portion forever.... As for me, the nearness of God is my good;
I have made the Lord GOD my refuge.

PSALM 73:26, 28 NASB

You have no strength but what God gives, and you can have all the strength that God can give.

ANDREW MURRAY

Not one word of all the good promises the Lord your God gave you has failed. Every promise has been fulfilled; not one has failed.

JOSHUA 23:14 NIV

God delights to show up when His children call on His name,
trusting fully in Him to come through.

FRANCIS CHAN

Let us hold unswervingly to the hope we profess,
for he who promised is faithful.

HEBREWS 10:23 NIV

*M*ost of the important things in the world have been accomplished by people who have kept on trying when there seemed to be no hope at all.

DALE CARNEGIE

My salvation and my honor depend on God; he is my mighty rock, my refuge. Trust in him at all times, you people; pour out your hearts to him, for God is our refuge.

PSALM 62:7-8 NIV

*Y*ou are a child of your heavenly Father. Confide in Him.
Your faith in His love and power can never be bold enough.

BASILEA SCHLINK

May the Lord direct your hearts into the love of God
and into the steadfastness of Christ.

2 THESSALONIANS 3:5 NASB

*E*very time I begin to feel that there just isn't any more strength in me,
I end up knowing that there is more…in Him.

GLORIA GAITHER

He said to me, "My grace is sufficient for you, for my power is made perfect in weakness." Therefore I will boast all the more gladly about my weaknesses, so that Christ's power may rest on me.

2 CORINTHIANS 12:9 NIV

I am so thankful, God, that You are here to help me,
to renew my dwindling strength. Just talking with You revives me.
Thank You that Your strength is enough for today.

MARILYN JANSEN

*G*od, who got you started in this spiritual adventure, shares with us the life of his Son and our Master Jesus. He will never give up on you. Never forget that.

1 CORINTHIANS 1:9 MSG

There will always be the unknown. There will always be the unprovable.
But faith confronts those frontiers with a thrilling leap.
Then life becomes vibrant with adventure!

ROBERT SCHULLER

*B*e strong, and let your heart take courage, all you who wait for the L_ORD_!

P_SALM_ 31 : 24 ESV

In case no one has told you today:
You are strong. You are brave. You are amazing.

MARGARET FEINBERG

I will be glad and rejoice in your love, for you saw my affliction and knew the anguish of my soul. You have not given me into the hands of the enemy but have set my feet in a spacious place.

PSALM 31:7-8 NIV

God changes caterpillars into butterflies, sand into pearls,
and coal into diamonds using time and pressure.

RICK WARREN

With God all things are possible.

MARK 10:27 NKJV

The Lord Jesus, who in His love is so unspeakably near us,
is the Almighty One with whom nothing is impossible.

ANDREW MURRAY

*B*e still before the LORD and wait patiently for him.

PSALM 37:7 ESV

I don't think there is anyone who needs God's help and grace
as much as I do. Sometimes I feel so helpless and weak.
I think that is why God uses me. Because I cannot depend
on my own strength, I rely on Him twenty-four hours a day.

MOTHER TERESA

God's peace...is far more wonderful than the human mind can understand. His peace will keep your thoughts and your hearts quiet and at rest.

PHILIPPIANS 4:7 TLB

*O*nly God gives true peace—a quiet gift He sets within us
just when we think we've exhausted our search for it.

*J*esus [said], "Anyone who is thirsty may come to me!
Anyone who believes in me may come and drink!
For the Scriptures declare, 'Rivers of living water will flow from his heart.'"

JOHN 7:37-38 NLT

When we do God's will and run His errands, we develop spiritual strength and are able to give to others out of our abundance.

A. E. SANNER

For you who revere my name, the sun of righteousness
will rise with healing in its rays.

MALACHI 4:2 NIV

I am convinced that God has built into all of us an appreciation of beauty and has even allowed us to participate in the creation of beautiful things and places. It may be one way God brings healing to our brokenness, and a way that we can contribute toward bringing wholeness to our fallen world.

MARY JANE WORDEN

The joy of the LORD is your strength.

NEHEMIAH 8:10 NKJV

Give God your waning thoughts. Question Him about the hard parts.
Seek His mercy. Seek His strength.

MAX LUCADO

Ellie Claire® Gift & Paper Expressions
Franklin, TN 37067
EllieClaire.com
Ellie Claire is a registered trademark of Worthy Media, Inc.

Courage, Dear Heart Journal
© 2015 by Ellie Claire
Published by Ellie Claire, an imprint of Worthy Publishing Group,
a division of Worthy Media, Inc.

ISBN 978-1-63326-051-1

Stock or custom editions of Ellie Claire titles may be purchased in bulk for educational,
business, ministry, fundraising, or sales promotional use. For information, please e-mail
info@EllieClaire.com

Compiled by Jill Jones

Printed in China

2 3 4 5 6 7 8 9 10 – 20 19 18 17 16 15